ALEX
KUSKOWSKI

A FUN AND CREATIVE INTRODUCTION TO FIBER ART

COOL
NEEDLE FELTING
for KIDS

WITHDRAWN

Checkerboard
Library

An Imprint of Abdo Publishing
www.abdopublishing.com

VISIT US AT WWW.ABDOPUBLISHING.COM

Published by Abdo Publishing, a division of ABDO, PO Box 398166,
Minneapolis, Minnesota 55439. Copyright © 2015 by Abdo Consulting
Group, Inc. International copyrights reserved in all countries. No part
of this book may be reproduced in any form without written permission
from the publisher. Checkerboard Library™ is a trademark and logo of
Abdo Publishing.

Printed in the United States of America, North Mankato, Minnesota
062014
092014

 THIS BOOK CONTAINS
RECYCLED MATERIALS

Design and Production: Anders Hanson, Mighty Media, Inc.
Series Editor: Liz Salzmann
Photo Credits: Anders Hanson, Shutterstock

The following manufacturers/names appearing in this book are
trademarks: Sharpie®

Library of Congress Cataloging-in-Publication Data
Kuskowski, Alex., author.
  Cool needle felting for kids : a fun and creative introduction to fiber
art / Alex Kuskowski.
    pages cm. -- (Cool fiber art)
  Audience: Ages 8-10.
  Includes index.
  ISBN 978-1-62403-309-4
1. Felt work--Juvenile literature. 2. Felting--Juvenile literature. I.
Title.
  TT849.5.K87 2015
  746.0463--dc23
                            2013043055

TO ADULT HELPERS

This is your chance to assist someone new to crafting! As children learn to craft they develop new skills, gain confidence, and make cool things. These activities are designed to help children learn how to make their own craft projects. Some activities may need more assistance than others. Be there to offer guidance when they need it. Encourage them to do as much as they can on their own. Be a cheerleader for their creativity.

Before getting started, remember to lay down ground rules for using the crafting tools and cleaning up. There should always be adult supervision when a child uses a sharp tool.

TABLE OF CONTENTS

Fun Felting

Discover how to make art with felt! Needle felting is the art of making things using felt. You can use needle felting to make beads, stuffed animals, or beautiful pictures.

You'll find a lot of ideas here to help you start needle felting. Step-by-step instructions make learning a breeze. You'll love to show off the things you make. Just turn the page and see how fun felting can be!

Tools of the Trade

NEEDLE FELTING FOAM PAD

A foam pad is used as a work surface for needle felting. It should be 2 inches [5 cm] thick and 8 inches [20 cm] square.

NEEDLE FELTING TOOLS

Felting needles are made of steel. They have little **barbs**. The barbs tangle the wool fibers. This makes the wool stick together when poked.

Needle felting tools hold the felting needles. Some tools hold one needle. Others hold more than one. We used a tool that holds three needles for the projects in this book.

Roving

Wool roving comes in many colors. It is used to finish shapes and projects.

YARN

Add detail to your projects with yarn. Make sure to use 100% wool yarn.

PATTERNS

Patterns for needle felting come with directions. Many also have pictures to follow along with. There are tons of fun patterns to choose from.

IT'S IN THE BAG

Keep a bag to hold your needle felting tools, roving, and general craft supplies like the ones below!

BAG

BEADS AND BUTTONS

PEN AND PAPER

MEASURING TAPE

FELTING NEEDLE

SAFETY PINS

SCISSORS

YARN

NEEDLES

GLUE

THREAD

ROVING

Basics

USING THE FELTING NEEDLE

Make sure needles are secure inside the felting needle tool. Follow the directions on the packaging.

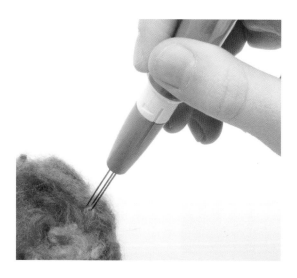

WARNING

Be careful! Felting needles are very sharp. Work slowly. Make sure you do not poke yourself.

Always put a foam pad or brush under the item you're working on.

The needles break easily. Hold the needle felting tool straight up and down.

Store needles safely when you're not using them. Try keeping them in a small box.

Felt it!

Cut a small section of roving.

Flatten out the roving with your hands.

Layer it evenly on a foam pad.

Push the needle down through the roving until it hits the foam pad. Pull it up. Repeat.

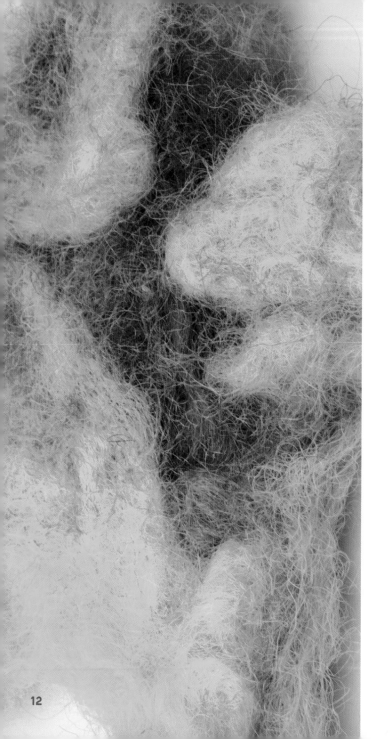

STARTING UP

GET STARTED ON BECOMING A FELTING STAR!

WHAT YOU NEED

NEEDLE FELTING TOOL, WOOL ROVING, COOKIE CUTTER, MEASURING TAPE, FOAM PAD

Put the cookie cutter in the middle of the foam.

 Put roving in the cookie cutter. Add small pieces until the layer of roving is 1 inch (2.5 cm) thick.

 Press the needle down inside the cookie cutter. Go through the roving into the foam. Pull it up. Repeat the pressing motion until the wool begins to hold together.

 Remove the cookie cutter. Poke the edges of the felt with a needle to **define** them. Add more roving if necessary.

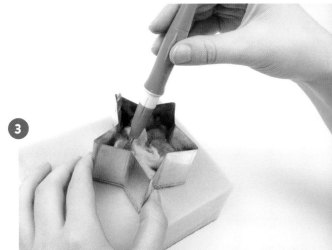

13

WORK OF ART

PAINT IT ON
WITH FELT!

WHAT YOU NEED

WOOL OR FELT HEADBAND,
WOOL ROVING, NEEDLE
FELTING TOOL, FOAM
PAD, PAPER, MARKER

 Draw your design on paper.

 Twist pieces of wool roving together until they look like yarn.

 Put the foam pad inside the headband. Lay the wool on the headband. Copy the design you drew.

 Begin needling the yarn. Needle it in place until the fibers stick together.

 Look at the back to check your work. If the yarn comes through evenly, it is done.

BEAD BRACELET LOOP

WHAT YOU NEED

WOOL ROVING (THREE COLORS), NEEDLE FELTING TOOL, FOAM PAD, SEWING NEEDLE, ELASTIC THREAD, GLUE

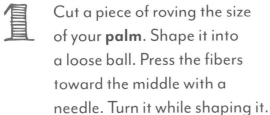

 Cut a piece of roving the size of your **palm**. Shape it into a loose ball. Press the fibers toward the middle with a needle. Turn it while shaping it.

 When the shape is a loose ball, hold it on the foam pad. Needle the ball while turning it slowly. Needle evenly around the entire shape.

 Make three balls with each color of roving.

 Thread the sewing needle with elastic thread. Thread the balls onto the elastic thread.

 Tie the ends of the thread together. Use a double knot. Put a drop of glue on the knot to secure it. Let the glue dry.

 Dress up the felt balls by adding yarn strands. Needle the yarn to keep it in place.

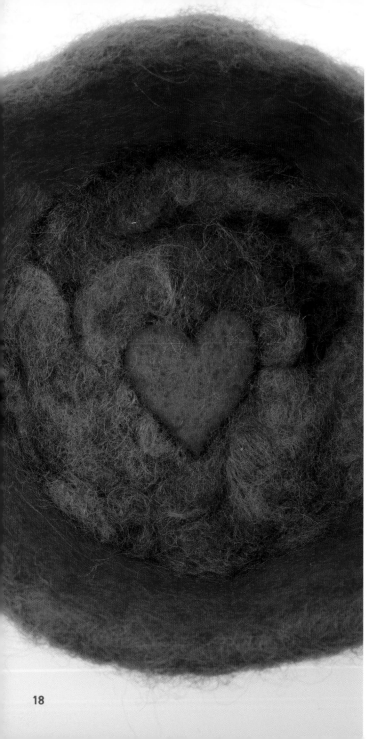

HIDDEN HEART BOWL

WHAT YOU NEED

FOAM 2 INCHES (5 CM) THICK, FOAM PAD, WOOL ROVING (TWO COLORS), NEEDLE FELTING TOOL, LIQUID DISH SOAP, TEASPOON, BOWL, DRINKING GLASS, RED FELT, MEASURING TAPE

1. Cut the foam into a circle 3 inches (7.6 cm) across. Cover a flat side with a ⅓-inch (.8 cm) layer of roving. Needle it flat.

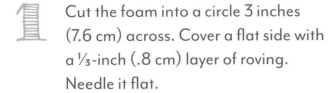

2. Wrap a second color of roving around the side. Make it ⅓ inch (.8 cm) thick. Needle it flat. Add more roving along the seam where the two colors meet. Needle the two colors together.

3. Take the roving off of the foam. Fill a bowl with hot water. Add 2 teaspoons of dish soap. Put the wool bowl in the water. Press the sides to shape it. When the wool bowl begins to shrink and become firm, take it out. Rinse it in cold water. Place it over the bottom of a drinking glass. Let it dry 24 hours.

4. Put the bowl back over the foam circle. Add roving to any uneven areas and needle it in.

5. Cut a heart out of felt. Set the wool bowl on a foam pad. Place the heart in the bottom of the bowl. Needle it into place.

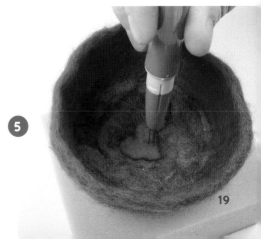

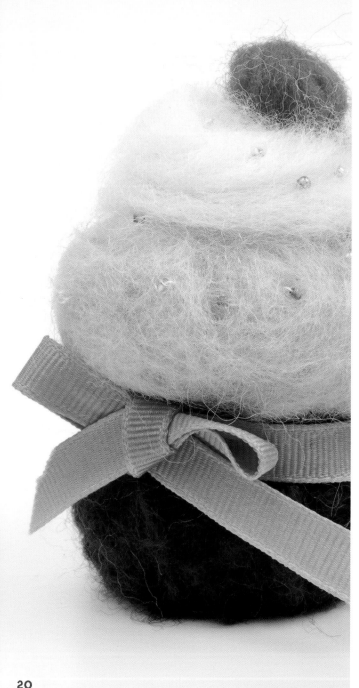

DELECTABLE CUPCAKE

WHAT YOU NEED

WOOL ROVING (FOUR
COLORS), NEEDLE
FELTING TOOL, FOAM
PAD, SCISSORS,
MEASURING TAPE

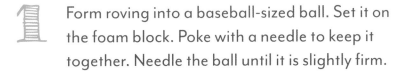

1. Form roving into a baseball-sized ball. Set it on the foam block. Poke with a needle to keep it together. Needle the ball until it is slightly firm.

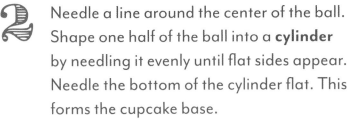

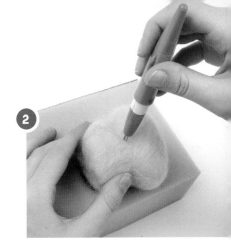

2. Needle a line around the center of the ball. Shape one half of the ball into a **cylinder** by needling it evenly until flat sides appear. Needle the bottom of the cylinder flat. This forms the cupcake base.

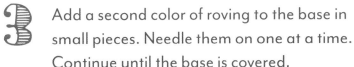

3. Add a second color of roving to the base in small pieces. Needle them on one at a time. Continue until the base is covered.

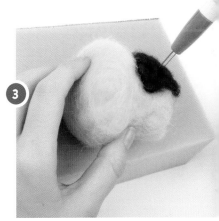

4. Separate out 6 inches (15 cm) of the third color of roving. Place it on top of the cupcake. Needle it in lightly. Make sure it is still **fluffy**.

5. Roll a piece of the fourth color of roving into a marble-sized ball. Needle it into shape.

6. Place the ball on top of the cupcake. Needle it where the ball meets the cupcake top.

TIP Add decorations!
Sew on beads for sprinkles.

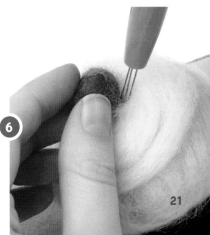

FELTED SUSHI MAGNETS

WHAT YOU NEED

WOOL ROVING (WHITE, RED, GREEN, YELLOW, AND BLACK), GREEN FELT, FABRIC GLUE, NEEDLE FELTING TOOL, FOAM PAD, 1-INCH (2.5 CM) MAGNET, HOT GLUE

1. Form a piece of green roving into a 1-inch (2.5 cm) ball. Needle it into a firm cube. Make a second cube with yellow roving.

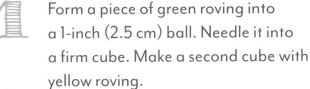

2. Roll a piece of red roving into an oval 2 inches (5 cm) long and 1 inch (2.5 cm) thick. Needle it into a rectangle.

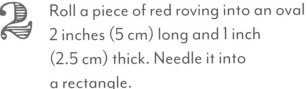

3. Place the cubes next to the rectangle. Needle them together. Needle them where the shapes meet.

4. Wrap a ¼-inch (.6 cm) layer of black roving around the shapes. Needle it in place. Wrap a thicker layer of white roving around the black roving. Needle it in place.

5. Cut a leaf out of green felt. Place it on the **sushi**. Needle it in.

6. Put a dot of hot glue on the leaf. Place the magnet on the glue. Let it dry.

7. Make more sushi magnets. Try different colors and shapes.

SNUGGLY PENGUIN

WHAT YOU NEED

WOOL ROVING (WHITE, BLACK, YELLOW), NEEDLE FELTING TOOL, FOAM PAD, FELT (WHITE AND BLACK), MEASURING TAPE

1. Roll a large piece of white roving into an oval. Place it on the foam pad. Needle it until it is dense. It should be about 2 inches (5 cm) long. Needle both ends of the oval flat. This is the penguin's body.

2. Roll and needle a ball about 1 inch (2.5 cm) across. This is the penguin's head.

3. Needle the head to one end of the body. Needle where the head and body meet.

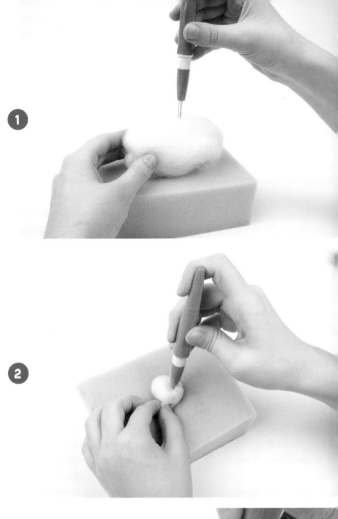

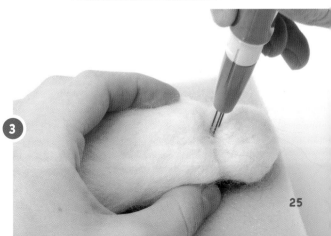

25

4 Cover one side of the body and head with black roving. Needle small pieces in one at a time.

5 Turn the penguin over. Cover the front of the head with black roving. Needle it in place.

6 Tear off a small piece of yellow roving. Needle it into a triangle. This is the penguin's beak.

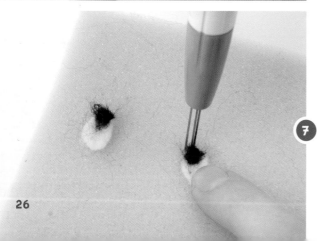

7 Cut two small circles out of white felt. Tear off two tiny pieces of black roving. Needle one onto each felt circle. These are the penguin's eyes.

Needle the eyes and beak onto the head. Needle them lightly.

 Cut two ovals out of black felt. They should be 1.5 inches (3.8 cm) long. Cut off one end of each oval so it's flat. These are the penguin's wings.

 Needle the flat end of one wing to the side of the body. Needle the other wing onto the other side.

 Tear off two small pieces of yellow roving. Needle them into small ovals. These are the penguin's feet. Needle them onto the bottom of the body.

8

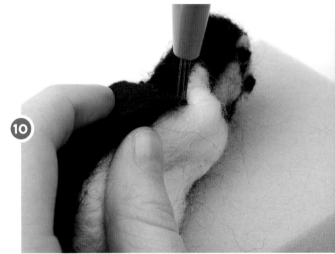

10

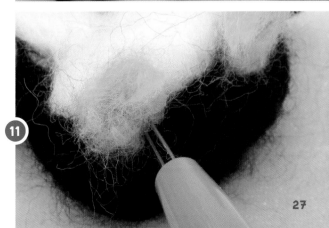

11

RUB-A-DUB SUDS

GET SOAPY
WITH FELT!

WHAT YOU NEED

WOOL ROVING (WHITE
AND BLACK), FOAM PAD,
NEEDLE FELTING TOOL,
BAR OF SOAP, BOWL,
MEASURING TAPE, TOWEL

1. Lay a ⅓-inch (.8 cm) layer of white roving on the foam pad. Make sure it's big enough to cover your bar of soap.

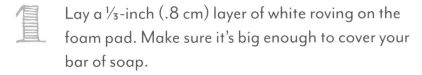

2. Place a small piece of black roving about 1 inch (2.5 cm) from the right edge. Needle the black roving into an oval shape. This is the sheep's face. Add small circles of black roving on either side of the oval. These are the ears.

3. Needle white roving to the face for eyes. Needle four small black rectangles about 1 inch (2.5 cm) from the bottom. These are the legs.

4. Needle a small black oval about 1 inch (2.5 cm) from the left side. This is the tail.

5. Wrap the roving around the soap. Cover the entire bar of soap with the roving. Make sure the sheep's features stay on the top of the soap. Arrange them near the edges.

6. Fill the bowl with hot water. **Scrub** and squeeze the soap underwater. Hold the roving around the soap. The roving will shrink to cover the soap. When the roving stops moving around the soap, squeeze out any extra water. Put the soap on a towel and let it dry for 3 hours.

Keep Needle Felting!

You can needle felt almost anything! You can make cool stuff for yourself. Or make gifts for family and friends. There are tons of ways to use needle felting.

Explore craft and fabric stores. Check out books on needle felting at the library. Look up needle felting tips and projects online. Get inspired and create your own designs. Try making a picture with needle felting. Felt decorations for your clothes. It's all about using your creativity!

GLOSSARY

BARB – a sharp point that sticks out and backward.

CYLINDER – a solid shape with two parallel circles bound by a curved surface. A soda can is a cylinder.

DEFINE – to make more distinct or clear.

DENSE – thick or crowded together.

FLUFFY – light, soft, and airy.

PALM – the inside of your hand between your wrist and fingers.

PATTERN – a sample or guide used to make something.

SCRUB – to rub hard.

SUSHI – a Japanese food made with rice, seafood, vegetables, and seaweed.

WEB SITES

To learn more about fiber art, visit ABDO online at www.abdopublishing.com. Web sites about creative ways for kids to make fiber art are featured on our Book Links page. These links are routinely monitored and updated to provide the most current information available.

INDEX